This book belongs to

Katie MANNERS

Nicky the Nature Detective
was first published in Sweden by Raben & Sjögren under
the title *Maja Tittar på Naturen*

William Collins Sons & Co Ltd
London · Glasgow · Sydney · Auckland
Toronto · Johannesburg

First published in Great Britain 1985
© text Ulf Svedberg 1983
© illustrations Lena Anderson 1983
concept Lena Anderson 1983
© this translation William Collins Sons & Co Ltd 1985
ISBN 0 00 195253-6
Printed in Italy

A Hot Day by A S J Tessimond is reproduced by permission
of Hubert Nicholson
Winter Morning by Ogden Nash is reproduced by permission
of Curtis Brown Ltd London and New York on behalf of the
estate of Ogden Nash copyright © 1961 by Ogden Nash

NICKY
THE NATURE DETECTIVE

pictures by Lena Anderson

text by Ulf Svedberg

translated by Ingrid Selberg

Collins

IN THE COUNTRYSIDE YOU NEED TO KEEP YOUR EYES OPEN...

Do come and meet Nicky. All through the year she loves to explore what is happening in the countryside. There's so much to look for and discover. Really, all you need is a good pair of eyes and ears.

In the springtime there are lots of birds to spot, while in the summer there are plenty of flowers and insects – in fact, there are so many you almost can't keep track of them. In autumn, Nicky observes migrating birds and looks for fruits and mushrooms. And the leaves on the trees turn such beautiful colours. Winter isn't quite so colourful, nor so full of plant and animal life as other times of the year, but there's still lots to see.

It's fun to follow what happens to one special tree throughout a whole year. Nicky has chosen a maple. Its leaves turn lovely rich colours in the autumn. The maple fruits, or helicopters, are fun too. But choose whichever tree you like best and go out exploring just like Nicky.

There's so much to find in nature – plants, animals and also their tracks and other clues they leave behind. You can find feathers, maybe some bones, even a whole skeleton, some hedgehog droppings in the garden, an owl pellet, or an unusual flower. It's fun to be a nature detective because there's so much to investigate.

But Nicky can't possibly show you everything – only a little bit of what she finds especially interesting.

Field guides to flowers and birds are very useful, and if you can get a pair of binoculars or a magnifying glass, they are a great help too.

At the back of the book there's a list of books for further reading if you want to learn more. They might tell you why birches grow witches' brooms, how the crossbill breeds in the midst of winter and if the earwig can *really* crawl into a person's ear. But meanwhile, have a good time with Nicky.

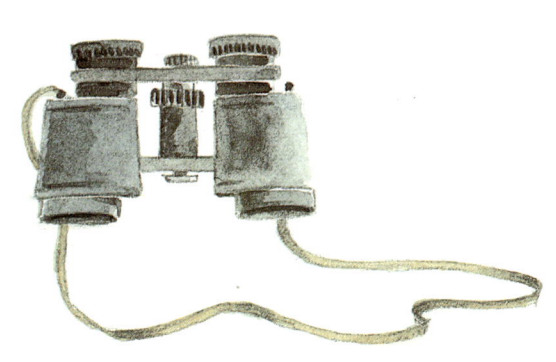

AND YOUR EARS TOO...

SPRING

This is the weather the cuckoo likes,
    And so do I;
When showers betumble the chestnut
  spikes,
    And nestlings fly:
And the little brown nightingale bills his
  best,
And they sit outside at 'The Travellers'
  Rest',
And maids come forth sprig-muslin drest,
And citizens dream of the south and west,
    And so do I.

Thomas Hardy

TREES
The maple tree flowers before it comes into leaf. But after a few days the leaf buds burst open and the pale green leaves appear. Some maples have reddish coloured leaves. Insects love sucking the nectar from the maple blossoms.

BIRDS
The male chaffinch sings and builds a nest. The nuthatch climbs headfirst down a tree (no other bird can do that!) and lays its eggs in a hole made by another bird. If the hole is too big, the nuthatch fills in the edges. The blackbird looks for earthworms on the lawn and the wagtail hops on the ground.

PLANTS
The celandine has almost finished blooming when the wood anemone appears like white carpets. In the evening the wood anemone closes its petals. Nicky tries an experiment to see if this is true. She puts an empty tin over a few open wood anemones for half an hour. It is dark inside the jar so the flowers are tricked into thinking it's evening. Half an hour later when Nicky checks, the flowers have closed their petals.

INSECTS
The few butterflies that Nicky can see in springtime have spent the winter in tree crevices or in lofts and cellars. Most butterflies die in the autumn after laying their eggs. The eggs, and sometimes the larvae, can survive the winter. Ants start to tidy up their anthills for the summer.

OTHER ANIMALS
The hedgehog comes out of hibernation and it is *very* hungry. It looks for earthworms and beetles to eat. It has about 16,000 hard prickles on its body. Baby hedgehogs are born with soft prickles. Thank heavens for that, thinks the mother hedgehog!

Trees

There are so many different kinds of trees. Some are tall and slender, others short and thick. Some have leaves that fall in the autumn, others have needles that stay on the tree throughout the winter. The larch is the only British conifer that loses its needles in the autumn.

The leaves grow in the spring. They suck up water from the ground to make food for the tree. If you break a twig a bit of liquid, called sap, oozes out. The tree is "bleeding". It soon stops and does not hurt the tree.

Most of the sunlight comes from the south. So trees often grow leaning southwards and with more branches in that direction. The tree's annual rings are wider on the south side.

The annual rings tell you a lot about the tree and whether it was a good or bad year for growth. The wider the rings, the more food the tree found and the more it grew.

Willow or sallow twigs take root easily in water. Nicky puts some in a jar and changes the water often. When the little root hairs have sprouted, she looks at them with a magnifying glass.

What's underneath the bark?
On dead trees or stumps you can easily pick away a piece of old bark. Hiding underneath you will find lots of creepy crawlies – millipedes, spiders, small beetles and ants. In the wood itself you can see patterns of tunnels made by beetles and other insects.

I CAN SEE YOU HAVE EXPERIENCED A GREAT DEAL

How old can a tree get?
The world's oldest tree is an American conifer, called the sequoia, which is 4600 years old. In Britain the oldest tree is a yew tree in Scotland, which is 2000 years old.

How tall can a tree grow?
The tallest tree in Britain is the Douglas fir and it grows to over 50 metres. But the world's tallest tree is the American redwood which is 126 metres tall.

Listen to the pine cones!
On a quiet winter's day Nicky can hear the pine cones popping. The seeds inside the cone are ripe and are being released. They sail off on little wings. The seeds land on the ground not far away and new pine trees start to grow.

How cones grow
Conifers have both male and female flowers. Pollen from the yellow male flower is carried by the wind and lands on the red female flower. It then grows into a green cone. When the cone is ripe, it turns brown. The scales open and the seeds are released. Some cones ripen in a year, but the Scots pine cone takes two years.

CAN YOU HEAR THE PINE CONES?

Why do birds sing?

ZEE IT, ZEE IT...

HEAVENLY!

Doesn't it sound lovely, thinks Nicky. But when a bird sings it's really a way for the male to say that he'd like to find a female. It is a courtship song. He is trying to attract females into his territory.

When the male has found a female they mate and build a nest. The male still sings but now it's to warn off other males: keep away!

When the young have hatched, he stops singing. He doesn't want to attract any other animals to the nest. The young need to be protected.

How old do birds become?
A bird lives a dangerous life. It can be eaten by an enemy, get caught in bad weather, starve, become ill, or fail to breed. Even if it survives these dangers, it doesn't grow very old. A little bird, such as a robin, great tit, sparrow or blue tit only lives about three years. The bigger the bird, the longer it tends to live.

The inhabitants of the nesting box
In springtime the birds give the nesting box a good clean out. They want it nice and tidy! Both the male and female help. When the nest is ready, the male sits outside singing and sometimes he helps the female to sit on the eggs. (This varies a bit depending on the kind of bird.) Small birds sit on their eggs for about three weeks before they hatch. The male brings food for the female and later for the chicks too. They need feeding many times an hour! If you're really lucky you might see the chicks leave the nesting box. Afterwards, they stay nearby and beg for food from their parents.

The cuckoo
The cuckoo is the only bird nesting in Britain that doesn't build its own nest. The female lays her eggs in another bird's nest. If the mother bird hatched in a pied wagtail's nest, she will lay her eggs in a pied wagtail's nest too. The cuckoo's egg is bigger than the wagtail's but otherwise exactly the same. The foster bird never notices a thing.

The cuckoo's egg develops more quickly than the foster parents' own eggs. When the cuckoo chick hatches, it shoves the other eggs and young out of the nest. The foster parents don't notice even if their own young are lying on the ground underneath the nest and cheeping.

The foster parents work very hard to feed the young cuckoo. It grows quickly and gets big. Sometimes the tiny parent has to sit on the young cuckoo's back to stuff food into its mouth.

Sleeping birds don't fall down
Birds don't fall off branches when they sleep. Their toes grip the branch automatically when they fall asleep. There is a tendon that "locks" the foot into place.

The Frog,

Springtime is the heyday of the frog. In March and April you can hear their croaking from ponds and ditches. The male grasps a female and clambers onto her back. Other males try to push him off.

The eggs are fertilized at the same moment as the female lays them in the water. They are covered with a jelly that swells up so that each egg looks like a round ball. After a few days you can see something black inside the egg. This is the tadpole.

About three weeks later there are small fishlike tadpoles with gills swimming about. The tadpoles grow quickly, their gills disappear and are replaced by lungs. They grow hind legs, followed by front legs. All the legs have webs between the toes. The tail shrinks and the tadpole has become a

the Toad, the Snake

little frog. It is ready to leave the water and live on land.

Many animals – water shrews, fish, some birds and snakes – love to eat frogs!

You can tell the difference between frogs' eggs, or spawn, and toad spawn. Frogs lay their eggs in clumps, while toads lay theirs in long winding ribbons.

What do frogs eat?
Tiny tadpoles scrape off algae growing on water plants. Larger tadpoles eat bits of the plants themselves and dead animals. Grown frogs like insects, earthworms, snails and even tadpoles! They are also good at catching flies with their long sticky tongues.

Raise a frog
Take a large bowl or aquarium. Place a layer of clean sand on the bottom and add some pond water. Anchor some water plants in the sand with small stones. Put in a little frogspawn. When the tadpoles hatch feed them on lettuce and nettle leaves. When legs appear they will also take meat. Dangle a piece of raw meat on thread so you can remove it when they have finished. Baby frogs will want to leave the water, so float a piece of wood in the bowl. You should then return them to the pond. The water should be changed if it starts to smell.

Toads don't jump like frogs, they crawl because they are slower. Their skin is rough with warts on it, while frogs have smooth skin. Nicky finds it's not hard to tell them apart.

Snakes don't have ears but they can feel vibrations in the ground when someone is coming. Then they slither away. Grass-snakes and slow-worms are completely harmless. Nicky leaves all snakes alone. They are useful because they hunt shrews and mice.

Look at the frog

FIRST AN EGG... THEN A TADPOLE... THAT GROWS LEGS... ITS TAIL SHRINKS... ALL COMPLETE! UP ON LAND!

Flowers

The flower
To our eyes most flowers are beautifully coloured, but insects see them differently. Inside the flower is the pistil and stamen which are necessary for the plant to reproduce itself.

The leaves
All green plants can make their own food. Using water from the soil, carbon dioxide from the air, sunshine and chlorophyll (the green substance in the leaves) they make a nutritious sugar and oxygen.

WHEN YOU PICK A FLOWER, DON'T PULL IT UP BY THE ROOTS OR THERE MIGHT NOT BE ANY NEXT YEAR!

The stalk
lifts the leaves and flowers up to the light. It stands up against bad weather and wind, even if it looks spindly.

The roots
hold the plant firmly in the ground and also draw up nutrients (minerals) from the soil with their fine hairs.

and Bees

HERE ARE THE GRAINS OF POLLEN

Think how many lovely flowers there are and what lovely colours: red, yellow, white and blue. Oddly enough, we are almost the only animals who can see these colours and the plants don't care about us. They only want to attract insects to themselves, nothing else.

Insects don't see colours the way we do. There is another kind of light, called ultraviolet, which we can't see but insects can. Some plants have secret signs to help flying insects to find them. These signs show up on photographs taken in ultraviolet light.

Insects fly from flower to flower. Pollen sticks to their hairy bodies and a little of it brushes off on the next flower they visit. Only pollen from a cowslip can make another cowslip produce seeds.

Flowers attract insects with their nectar. Sometimes we say that bees and other insects are looking for honey, but really they are after nectar. They swallow the nectar and it is changed into honey inside a special honey stomach. Then the bee spits up the honey and stores it in a cell in the honeycomb. Nicky doesn't think it sounds too appetizing but she likes brown bread and honey.

The bee brushes the grains of pollen off its body and makes them into a little ball stuck together with some honey. The pollen is stowed away between the hairs on the bee's hind legs, in the pollen basket. You can spot bees doing this if you keep your eyes open.

In the spring good plants for bees are coltsfoot, celandine, sallow and fruit tree blossoms, also blackthorn and oak flowers.

Some plants let the wind do the job of spreading their seeds. Pine trees, grasses, dandelions and willow herb are good examples.

In the spring Nicky sometimes sneezes and sneezes, her eyes run, her nose and throat itch. This is caused by an allergy to pollen called hay fever, which is very common. Many people are very sensitive to grass pollen and sometimes develop asthma or eczema.

YES, IT'S TRUE — BEES SPIT UP HONEY

What

When buds burst open

In the autumn the horse chestnut stops growing. At the tip of each twig there is a large pointed bud with a brown sticky covering. Sometime in April or May the bud begins to open. The sticky covering which protected the bud during the winter, leaves a scar on the twig when it falls off. Try to see if you can spot them. You can tell how much a twig has grown in a year by the distance between the two scars. This is different from the "horseshoe" leaf scar.

Take a twig and place it in a jar filled with water just as Nicky has done. You can do it with any type of tree but the horse chestnut is especially good because it has large buds which are easy to see.

What happens to buds during the year?
Tie a little ribbon round a hazel, birch, oak, beech or ash twig so that you can recognize it. Take a look at it regularly during the year until the tree loses its leaves. Draw it and measure how much it has grown.

Sow a seed
Plant some peas in plain soil in a flowerpot. (Yellow peas are good but so are green peas or runner beans.) Sow lots of them. Then it won't matter if you dig up one or two to have a look at the roots.

happens to buds and seeds?

When a pea grows, it sucks up water and swells. The seed coat splits open and a little root emerges. The root comes first and it grows downwards to help hold the new plant in the soil.

In the tip of the root there is a "cap" which protects the sensitive tip from damage. Behind lie lots of thin root hairs which take up water and minerals from the ground.

When the root is growing properly, the shoot begins to grow upwards into the air. This will become the stalk which carries the leaves and flowers, and finally the fruit.

...IT WAS QUICKER THAN I THOUGHT!

How does the water reach the leaves?

Trees and flowers need lots of water to make food for the tree. An average birch tree needs 400–600 litres of water every day during a warm summer.

But how does the water get from the roots to the top of a tall tree? Water comes up from the roots, through the trunk and along the branches to the leaves. The leaves are full of tiny holes through which the water evaporates and the new water is constantly replacing the water that has evaporated.

AMAZING! 600 LITRES!

THE WATER LILY TRICK
Try this trick of Nicky's. Pick a water lily leaf with a long stalk. Place the leaf under water and blow through the stalk. The air will pass through the tiny holes in the leaf and make bubbles on the surface. If air can get through these holes, then so can water! Water passes through tiny tubes inside all plants.

THE TULIP TRICK
Put a white tulip in a glass of water with some green (or other) food colouring in it. After a few hours the tulip petals will have green streaks. The water has carried the colouring with it up into the flower.

THE LEAF TRICK
Tie a clear plastic bag round a leafy twig on a tree. Soon you will see lots of drops of water inside the bag. This is water that has evaporated through the little holes in the leaves.

WATER AND FOOD COLOURING

NOW WE'LL SOON SEE

SUMMER

A Hot Day

Cottonwool clouds loiter.
A lawnmower, very far,
Birrs. Then a bee comes
To a crimson rose and softly
Deftly and fatly crams
A velvet body in.

A tree, June-lazy, makes
A tent of dim green light.
Sunlight weaves in the leaves,
Honey-light laced with leaf-light,
Green interleaved with gold.
Sunlight gathers its rays
In sheaves, which the wind unweaves
And then reweaves – the wind
That puffs a smell of grass
Through the heat-heavy, trembling
Summer pool of air.

A. S. J. Tessimond

TREES
The maple's flowers have long since fallen off and the leaves have turned dark green. You can hardly see the branches and twigs for all the leaves. Down on the ground it is shady and cool. Nicky loves to sit there.

BIRDS
It isn't so easy to see birds amidst all the greenery. Is there still someone in the nesting box? Great tits, blue tits or starlings may even have started a second brood of young.

PLANTS
Not all flowers are brightly coloured. There are lots of grasses which have small, pale flower heads. In the meadows you might find daisies, clover, thistles, poppies and buttercups. Nicky dries buttercups. They are still yellow and lovely in the wintertime. There are masses of dandelions – both flowers and seed heads – and Nicky picks the young leaves for salad. Stinging nettles flourish and are the favourite food of many caterpillars. Luckily the nettles don't sting their mouths!

INSECTS
The peacock and small tortoiseshell butterflies settle on the nettle leaves to lay their eggs because this is the food plant of their caterpillars. Other insects are multiplying as well. The place is swarming with them!

OTHER ANIMALS
In the grass you can hear shrews squeaking. The hedgehog has had her young. They follow behind their mother in a long line when they go out for an evening stroll. Give them a little water in a bowl. Be kind to hedgehogs – there aren't that many of them.

Buzzing, singing, chirping,

Insects make an incredible variety of sounds. Mosquitoes keep Nicky awake at night with their whining. But it's even worse when they are silent because then she knows they're about to bite! Fat flies buzz in the sunlight on the verandah especially when there's juice and buns for tea. Nicky tries to chase them away but it isn't easy to kill a fly. They have compound eyes made up of tiny eyes and can see movement more clearly than we can. They notice as soon as you get ready to strike a blow.

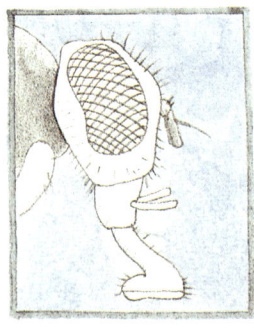

IF THE FLY WAS THIS SIZE YOU COULD SEE ALL ITS COMPOUND EYES AND MOUTH PARTS CLEARLY

Flies are unpleasant and spread disease everywhere. They can be found wherever there is dung, dead animals and excrement. The fly also deposits saliva on what it is going to eat. Set out a little bit of sugar and watch how the fly eats it. Its mouth is like a sucking pad that unfolds and works almost like a vacuum cleaner.

Mosquitoes lay their eggs in the water. When they hatch out, the larvae stay near the surface of the water. But when there is danger, they swim down towards the bottom. In warm climates mosquitoes can carry a dangerous disease called malaria.

In the summer we hear the crickets and grasshoppers singing away all day long. They live in the long grass and are at their loudest at the end of the summer when the young ones join in.

It is the males that sing. Grasshoppers rub their hind legs against their wing sheaths and crickets rub their wing sheaths together. Different types have different songs and you can learn to tell them apart. The females listen with interest. Their ears, by the way, are on their forelegs! But why not – flies have their sense of taste on their front feet.

How can you tell a grasshopper and a cricket apart? Grasshoppers have short antennae and bush crickets have long ones. The female bush cricket has a long sword-like egg laying tube.

THE GREEN BUSH CRICKET HAS LONG ANTENNAE...

and whining

...AND THE GRASSHOPPER HAS SHORT ANTENNAE

Bites and stings

Mosquitoes
The mosquito sucks blood with a "sucking" tube which pierces the skin like a sharp needle. Only the female sucks blood, the male sticks to plant juices! But the female needs blood for her eggs to develop properly.

It usually itches after a mosquito bite. The mosquito injects a liquid into the blood that prevents it from clotting quickly. Don't kill the mosquito. Let it finish sucking because then it will remove most of the liquid, and the bite won't itch so much.

Bees and wasps
You might get stung by a bee or a wasp. The sting swells up and hurts a little. This is what happens when a bee stings. The bee has a sting in the tip of its abdomen. It looks like two saws with barbs and a dagger between the blades. The saws make a hole and the knife sticks in and presses in the poison. The bee gets stuck and when it flies away the sting remains in the sore.

The wasp doesn't have such strong barbs

on its sting and therefore can pull it out again. The bee dies after stinging, but the wasp survives.

Ants

Ants can also bite. The small red ants have a little sting with which they inject poison. The ordinary wood ant doesn't have a sting but it can bite. It sprays formic acid with the tip of its abdomen and the spurt can reach 50 cm away. Hold your hand over the hill and take a smell!

Flies

There are some especially unpleasant flies that sting. In the summer when it is warm and damp horseflies, gadflies, midges and clegs appear. They are so silent that you don't notice them until they bite.

Stinging nettles

Nettle leaves and stalks are covered with hairs with sharp tips. They break easily and the tip pierces the skin injecting poisonous liquid. It stings but it isn't dangerous. Fresh young nettles make a delicious soup but Nicky always wears gloves when picking them!

Most insect bites and stings only hurt for a short time, then the pain goes away. You can bathe the wound in ammonia or vinegar. It helps to rub raw onion on a bee sting because the onion contains a substance that destroys bee poison. Try rubbing yourself with parsley to keep mosquitoes away.

Wild plants that

Thousands of years ago all plants were wild. Now we cultivate many of them for food: wheat, rye, maize, oats, potatoes and vegetables.

But we can eat wild plants too. However, don't pick them along the roadside because they will be polluted from car exhaust.

WARNING!

Make sure that you look everything up in a field guide so that you are *absolutely sure* you aren't eating anything poisonous. These berries are dangerous and should *never* be eaten: deadly nightshade, woody nightshade, yew, cuckoo pint. Check them in your flower book.

IT'S LUCKY I BROUGHT MY FIELD GUIDE ALONG...

GOOD PLANTS

Elm The fruit of the elm tree tastes good in a green salad.

Silverweed grows on the beach. The young leaves can be eaten in a salad.

Dandelion leaves that grow in the dark (e.g. under an old board) are especially delicious.

Cress There are many kinds. Water cress is especially tasty, but only pick it from fast-flowing, clear streams.

Red clover The bees take the nectar, but we can gather the leaves and eat them in salad.

Yarrow The tiny, delicately lobed leaves can be used as a slightly bitter herb to put on food.

Polypody fern sometimes grows on old stone walls. Its root tastes like liquorice.

you can eat

GOOD BERRIES

There are lots of good berries to eat, but there are also poisonous ones that you must learn to recognize.

Wild strawberries, wild raspberries, bilberries and blackberries are all delicious. Cloudberries, which grow in boggy moorlands are more rare. Some people say that they are the best of all.

Red whortleberries ripen in the autumn. Most berries can be eaten fresh but rowan berries are best if they are made into a jelly.

Have you tried threading wild strawberries on a piece of grass? If you place an unripe berry at the bottom the rest won't fall off.

GOOD LEAVES

Leaves can be used to make tea. They are dried and then crumbled to bits. Many plants make good teas: birch, rowan, hawthorn, wild strawberry, rose bay, and meadow sweet. From the garden, blackcurrant, strawberry, apple and pear leaves make good tea. Fir and pine trees can also be used to make tea but then you need to gather fresh needles and crush them in a mortar.

... OR ELSE I'D HAVE GOT A TUMMY ACHE!

Small woodland mammals

What is a mammal?
Most animals vary their body temperature according to the outside temperature. But birds and mammals have the same temperature more or less all the time.

Mammals give birth to living young which are fed on their mother's milk. They have hair on their bodies (some less than others – for example, human beings) and usually four legs. Whales, which aren't fish as some people think, have no legs at all.

are more beasts of prey too. Most rodents are small, such as rats and mice and the grey squirrel, but the beaver is a rodent too.

Some common mammals
Field voles are common in meadows. In particularly cold winters they make long tunnels under the snow and line them with dried grass. Nicky sometimes finds these "grass baskets" on the ground when the snow has gone.

THE FIELD VOLE HAS A SHORT TAIL...

...WHILE THE FIELD MOUSE HAS A LONG TAIL

Here are some small mammals that you and Nicky might see:

Rodents
There are many mammals in the woods and fields, and most of them are rodents. They have only two front teeth in their upper jaw.

Rodents are an important source of food for many larger animals and birds of prey. In years when there are many rodents, there

All voles have quite short tails.

The water vole, Britain's largest vole, lives where it is damp. It mostly eats reeds.

The field mouse is active mostly at night. It lives at the edge of the woods or in glades or thickets. It mainly eats seeds, nuts and acorns. In the winter it likes to come into the house.

The house mouse is a little smaller than the field mouse and lives indoors. Even the

MY GUINEA PIG IS A RODENT TOO

PLEASE GOD, LET ME SEE A SHREW!

brown rat comes into the house – an unwelcome guest!

The shrew is not a rodent
Shrews look like small mice but are related to hedgehogs and moles. They have long pointy noses and are heard more than they are seen. If you hear a squeaking in the grass, it is probably a shrew.

The hare and the rabbit
Hares and rabbits have teeth like rodents but they aren't closely related to them. Hares and rabbits produce droppings which can be seen all over their territory, especially around rabbit warrens. They pass two kinds. We see only the second. The first dropping is greenish and is eaten by the rabbit or hare as it contains vitamins.

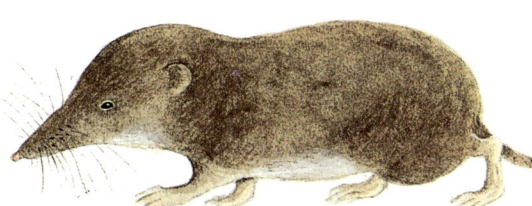

THIS IS WHAT A SHREW LOOKS LIKE

How wonderful to lie on your stomach on a little dock and peer down into the water! There's so much to look for – lots of small fishes and small animals.

Make an underwater viewer just like Nicky's. Take a large metal tin and remove the top and the bottom. Place the tin in a clear plastic bag and put a strong rubber band round it near the top to hold it tight. Place the bottom in the water and look through the open end. The plastic will bend in a little like a magnifying glass.

I'VE MADE AN UNDERWATER VIEWER

In this picture you can see Nicky fishing. It's fun to fish in the rain because the fish bite a lot then. But does it hurt the earthworm when you put it on the hook? Apparently not. No one has been able to find a sense organ for pain in an earthworm.

Right away you get a bite and up comes a perch. On its back it has sharp fins to defend itself against other fish that might try to eat it.

You can see how a fish breathes. Behind its mouth, at the sides of its head, are the gills. They are hidden behind gill covers.

The fish breathes/gulps water in through its open mouth. It closes its mouth and squeezes out the water through its gills. The gills take in the oxygen from the water that the fish needs to breathe.

In front of the back fin beneath the body there is a little hole. This is where the fish's droppings come out into the water. They fall on the bottom and are changed into fertilizer for the plants.

At the water's edge

Plants along the bank

Reeds grow along the edge of ponds and streams where the water is full of nutrients. The common reed is a type of grass – Britain's tallest and one of the tallest in the world. It can grow to five metres in height but then it usually stands a metre deep in the water.

Reedmace, with its brown "cigars", grows along with the common reed. Those strange cigars are really flowers! Each cigar can have more than 100,000 tiny flowers on it. In late winter the cigars burst and release masses of winged fruits over the water.

. . . and animals

The water is teeming with animals! Beneath the surface snails crawl. Whirligig beetles spin (on top of the surface) together with pond skaters. And there are many more . . .

Look at the perch

SPINY FINS ARE GOOD FOR SELF DEFENCE

THE FISH SWIMS WITH ITS TAIL FINS AND STEERS WITH ITS OTHER FINS

THIS IS WHERE THE DROPPINGS COME OUT

THE GILLS ARE UNDERNEATH THE GILL COVER

The life of a dragonfly

Nicky wishes that she could fly like a dragonfly. It's amazing! It can hover, fly backwards or glide. You can hear its wings rustling when they bump into each other.

There are many kinds of dragonfly, each more beautiful than the other. The back of its body has especially striking markings.

Two dragonflies can fly attached together while they are mating. The male attaches the tip of his tail behind the female's head and

she bends her tail forward onto the male's body where he has his mating organs.

When they have mated, she lays her eggs. Some dragonflies drop them into the water while they are flying, but others lay their eggs in moss or damp earth on land. Other kinds crawl into the water and attach their eggs to plants underneath the surface.

It takes the larvae of some types of dragonfly several years to become an adult dragonfly. The larva crawls up out of the water onto a reed. Its skin splits down the back and the dragonfly pulls itself out. Its old larval skin remains on the stalk. Its wings unfold and dry, then it flies away. It lives only a couple of months.

Dragonflies hunt small flying insects. They have small territories just as birds do.

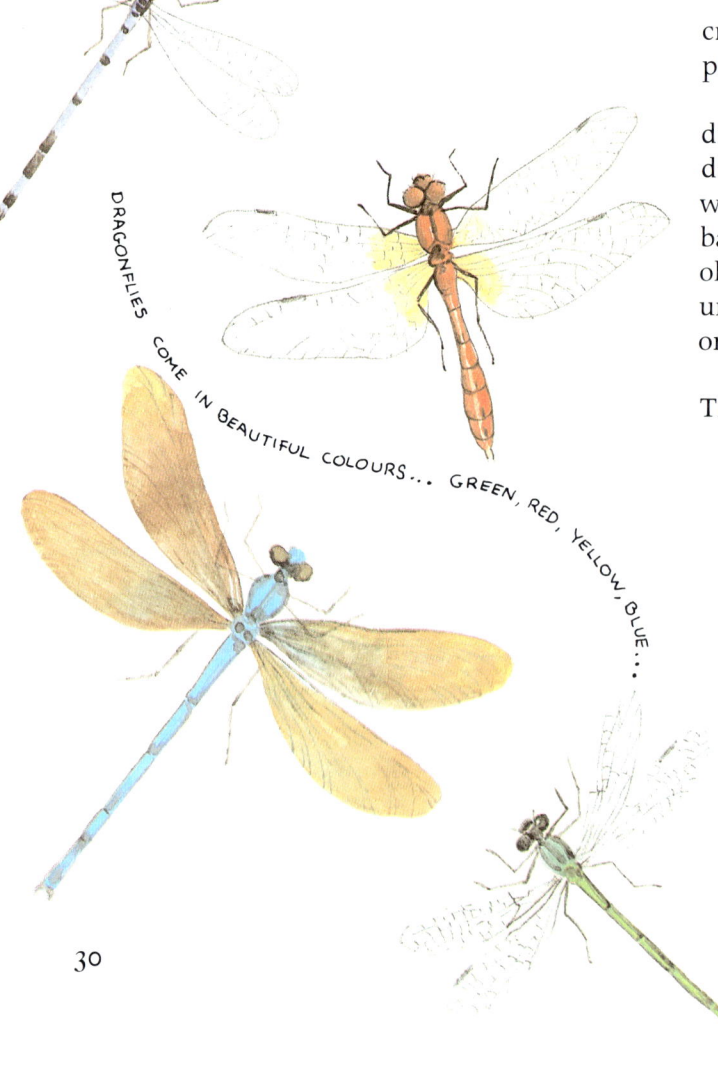

DRAGONFLIES COME IN BEAUTIFUL COLOURS... GREEN, RED, YELLOW, BLUE...

AUTUMN

This is the weather the shepherd shuns,
    And so do I;
When beeches drip in browns and duns,
    And thresh, and ply;
And hill-hid tides throb, throe on throe,
And meadow rivulets overflow,
And drops on gate-bars hang in a row,
And rooks in families homeward go,
    And so do I.

Thomas Hardy

TREES
The maple leaves have turned yellow, orange and red. Nicky presses and dries some leaves and makes pictures with them. Some maple leaves have large black spots on them which are fungus. Can you see any "helicopters" left on the tree?

BIRDS
Swallows sit on telephone wires. They are on their way to warmer places. The chaffinch looks for insects and seeds on the ground. Starlings are in their winter outfits; they no longer have the shiny spots that they had in the spring. The blackbird remains behind and pulls an earthworm out of the ground.

PLANTS
The celandine leaves are dark green and have started to wither round the edges, the hedgerows are bright with orange rosehips and dark red hawthorn berries. Most flowers have withered and disappeared.

INSECTS
The peacock and small tortoiseshell butterfly are both still about but soon they will look for a place to shelter for the winter. There aren't very many insects left, apart from a few lazy wasps.

OTHER ANIMALS
When it grows colder, the grass is wet with dew in the morning. Suddenly you can see all the spider's webs, those treacherous traps for insects. Slugs and garden snails are still crawling about. Slugs need to be careful because hedgehogs eat them with great enthusiasm.

A field vole rustles in the grass. It had better watch out for the buzzard, who is very fond of voles!

What happens to seeds and

What is a fruit and what is a seed? Well, a fruit is the part of the flower that contains the seed. Some fruits are soft and taste good: strawberries and raspberries – the crunchy bits are the seeds. Fruits can also be hard and dry; hazelnuts, beechnuts and sweet chestnuts, although you can eat what's inside them. Nuts are good and pigs and deer like acorns and beechnuts. Squirrels bury hoards of acorns.

How are seeds spread?
The wind is a good way of spreading seeds. Blow a dandelion "clock" so that the seeds sail through the air like parachutes, each with a tiny aviator hanging below.

Animals help to disperse seeds too. Birds, such as blackbirds and starlings, eat soft fruits. The seeds come out in their droppings. Animals can get seeds with hooks or burrs stuck on their fur: dogs come home with burdocks on them. Ants carry off small seeds and help to spread them too.

Why do trees and shrubs lose their leaves in autumn?
Leaves give out water vapour through their tiny holes all the time. In the winter when the ground is frozen, trees and shrubs get very little water through the roots. If the leaves remained, the tree might lose all its water and die.

What about fir and pine trees then? Their leaves – needles – remain throughout the winter. But needles are narrow and covered with a waxy coating so less water escapes from them.

What happens when a leaf falls off?
The tree seals up the area where the leaf stalk was attached to the branch so that neither water, insects nor fungus can enter. (In the picture of the horse chestnut on pages 14 and 15 you can see this triangular leaf scar.)

where do all the leaves go?

Where do all the leaves go?
There are masses of leaves. A football field covered with leaves would weigh about 1000 kilos! But by springtime most of them have disappeared. Where do they go?

Earthworms dispose of a lot of them. They drag them down into their tunnels under the ground and eat them up. Earthworms are more interesting than you think. Nicky likes to listen to them. Try it yourself! Let an earthworm crawl across a piece of paper and you will hear the scratching of its tiny bristles. If you use a magnifying glass, you can see them clearly. Have a look! The earthworm uses its bristles to brace itself against the walls of its tunnels. When a blackbird pulls a worm up out of the ground you can see the worm stretching out – it is holding on with its bristles.

DO YOU KNOW WHAT I FOUND IN A LITTLE SQUARE THIS BIG IN A WOOD?

LISTEN!

It's not only earthworms that eat leaves. In a 10 centimetre (4 inch) square of a woodland floor Nicky found:

3 SLUGS
14 MILLIPEDES
23 INSECTS AND THEIR LARVAE
120 BIG EARTHWORMS
217 WOODLICE
635 SPIDERS
63,000 TINY WORMS
30,000,000 BACTERIA

If these creatures covered a whole football field they would weigh about 5000 kilos. It's not so surprising that all the dead leaves disappear before spring comes.

Insy winsy spider

It's amazing how many people dislike spiders. They think that spiders are poisonous and that they bite. Both things are true, but not to people. It is only flies and insects that need worry. There are lots of different kinds of spiders in Britain – about 650 kinds. Some of them spin fine webs but most don't make any webs at all. They either chase their prey or ambush it from behind.

Spiders and webs
Autumn is the best time to see spiders' webs. When the meadow is wet with dew, Nicky can see all the different webs stretched between the bushes and the blades of grass. Some look like wheels, others are like thick covers. When the dew dries up, you can't see the webs any more. They really are death traps for insects.

Spiders have spinnerets on the undersides of their bodies. They start by spinning a frame. There are sticky strands for catching careless insects and dry ones for the spider to travel along.

Only the female spider spins a web. She has a kind of oil on her feet so that she won't get caught in her own web.

Spider's web thread is very thin, only 1/200 of a millimetre thick, but it is made up of many strands and is therefore very strong.

The spider's courtship
The female spider is nearly always hungry. She sees every animal that approaches her web as a possible meal. Even male spiders that come to mate with her! So the male has to get her in a good mood, or else he'll be eaten up. Some types of spiders mate with no problems. The male vibrates the web which attracts the female. Among other types the male ties up the female before he mates with her, just to be safe!

Spiders can fly
but without wings. In the autumn the spiderlings journey through the air. They sit

THIS IS HOW A SPIDER SPINS ITS WEB BETWEEN THE BLADES OF GRASS

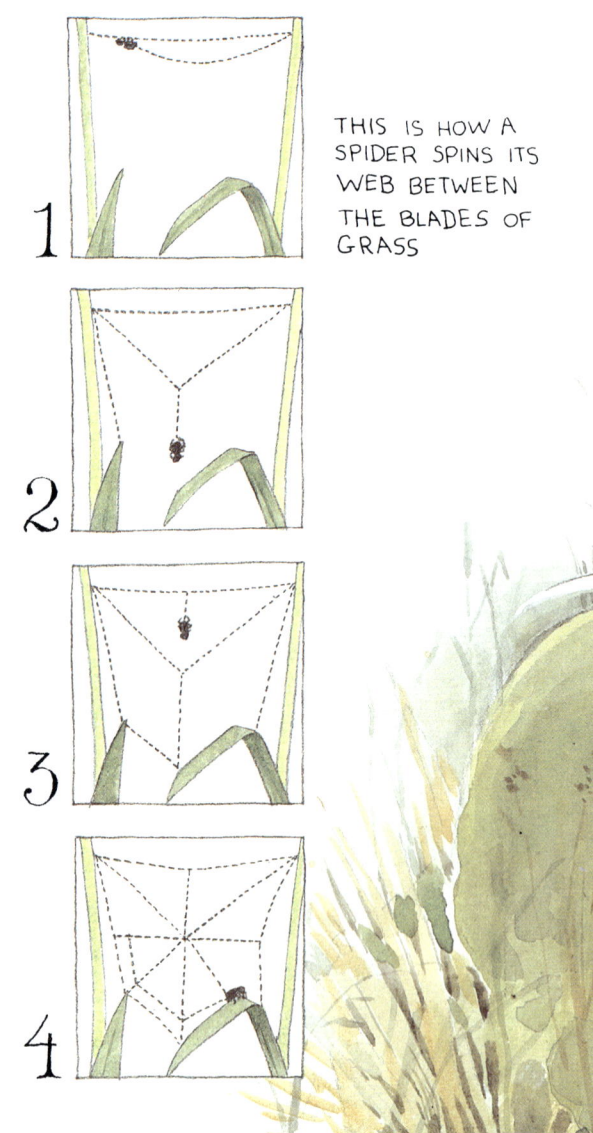

1
2
3
4

on a branch and spin a long thread which catches the wind. It is like a voyage in a balloon, where the spider can adjust the height by letting out more thread or taking it in. If it is very windy, the wind carries the young spiders far away. This is how spiders have journeyed all over the world and spread to new areas.

Animals

How do animals survive the winter? The weather can grow very cold and there is little food available. Some birds travel, or migrate, to warmer climates, while some other animals go to sleep or into hibernation. Animals that are staying through the winter gather food and store it away to eat later. They also grow thick coats to help keep them warm. Some insects spend the winter underneath tree bark, but others, before they die, lay eggs that survive the winter.

The hedgehog goes into hibernation. It searches for a safe place to spend the winter. Then it makes a nest of leaves, maybe dug into the compost or in the roots of a hedge. This keeps the hedgehog well protected from the cold.

When an animal hibernates, its temperature drops and it breathes so slowly that you can hardly notice it. The hedgehog takes a breath every five minutes. Its heart beats only a few times a minute.

The badger does not hibernate. In bad weather it goes to sleep in its sett, which is a deep burrow in the ground. Sometimes generations of badgers have lived in the same sett. If the weather grows mild, it wakes up, leaves the sett and goes out for a ramble.

The bear also dozes in a winter den. It gives birth to its young in the den during the winter.

Animals that doze in winter hideouts breathe normally and retain their usual body temperature. They can be woken up immediately although they might be in a bad mood! There's an old saying, "Never wake a sleeping bear."

Mice and voles gather a store of food throughout the autumn: nuts, acorns, apple seeds, grains of corn are put away in holes in the ground. They don't sleep in winter, but scamper about, even under the snow. You can often spot their tracks in the snow.

in Autumn

(Shrews behave like mice and voles.) Squirrels also hide away nuts here and there.

The hare's fur grows thicker in winter. In Scotland the mountain hare turns completely white. So does the stoat with only a black tip to its tail. In southern Britain the common hare remains brown all the year round.

Birds that don't migrate must hunt for food all day long. The days grow shorter and colder and the nights colder still. Many small birds die. They freeze to death or starve from lack of food. Nicky sets up a bird table in the garden for them.

Snakes, frogs and toads look for a safe place to hide away from the frost. Toads wait for the warmth of spring while deep in the ground or under a pile of wood.

Frogs often bury themselves into the mud at the bottom of a pond. They take in oxygen from the water through their skins.

Sometimes you can find adders and grass snakes curled up in a burrow together.

The ladybird hides itself in a crack in a tree, a tuft of grass or among leaves. It isn't fussy.

You can find peacock and small tortoiseshell butterflies in attics, cellars and woodsheds. They sleep with folded wings. Crickets and grasshoppers die before winter comes, but they have already laid their eggs, which will grow into new insects in the spring.

Snails retreat to a sheltered, frost-free place. They produce a foam made of lime at the opening of their shells. It hardens and seals the entrance so that they don't dry out. Slugs, which don't have shells, lay their eggs in the autumn and then die. The eggs hatch in the spring and the new slugs appear in the summer.

Why do birds migrate?

There are about 470 types of birds in Britain and about 40 of these are summer visitors. The rest stay in Britain throughout the cold months. The waxwing plucks rowan berries and the crossbill eats pine cones. The birds that eat insects need to go elsewhere when the insects die, otherwise they would starve to death.

But birds usually don't wait until the insects have disappeared before they depart. They set off far earlier. Birds, like animals and people, have chemicals called hormones in their bodies. The amount of hormones changes when the days grow shorter and the temperature lower. This change makes the birds eat all the time, storing fat in their bodies for the exhausting migration ahead. Then they set off. In the spring when the birds fly northwards again, their sex glands produce new hormones. Sometimes we say that birds have a "body clock" that tells them when to migrate.

Birds take quite a long time to travel to the south. Most of them fly at night. They use the daytime to look for food. Swallows and swifts fly with open mouths and catch insects while they are flying. When the birds return in the spring, they travel much more quickly.

Bird ringing
How do we know where birds migrate? Well, some scientists catch birds, place tiny aluminium rings, saying where the bird was caught and when, around their legs and release them. If you find a dead bird with a ring, you should send it to the address on the ring. This is how scientists who study birds learn about where they migrate.

Which birds migrate and which ones stay behind?

Sparrows — STAY WITH US ALL YEAR ROUND

Robins — ARE PERMANENT RESIDENTS

Wagtails — MIGRATE TO THE MEDITERRANEAN

Swallows — FLY ALL THE WAY TO SOUTHERN AFRICA

Nesting boxes

Autumn is a good time to put up new nesting boxes and empty out the old ones. Make sure that all the boxes are securely fastened. Nicky puts a little moss in the nesting box which makes it more comfortable for birds staying overnight.

Build a nesting box yourself! Take a piece of timber, about 2 cms thick, and 13 cms wide. Saw it as shown in the drawing below.

Screw a support on the back of the box so you can fasten it to a tree. Drill a hole 3 to 3·5 cms in diameter on the front. Arrange the pieces together to see if they fit and screw and glue them together. (You may need help!) This box would suit a tit, a flycatcher or a redstart.

Don't put a perch in front of the hole – this makes it easier for a cat to get at the young. Place nesting boxes facing south and east, and not too close together.

You can, of course, buy a nesting box instead.

SEE YOU AGAIN NEXT YEAR...

BUILDING A NESTING BOX ISN'T SO DIFFICULT WITH THE HELP OF AN ADULT. YOU TAKE A PIECE OF WOOD 150 CM LONG AND SAW IT LIKE THIS...

30	28	30	28	10	24
SIDE	SIDE	BACK	○ FRONT	FLOOR	ROOF

150

WINTER

Winter Morning

Winter is the king of showmen,
Turning tree stumps into snow men
And houses into birthday cakes
And spreading sugar over lakes.
Smooth and clean and frosty white,
The world looks good enough to bite.
That's the season to be young,
Catching snowflakes on your tongue.
Snow is snowy when it's snowing
I'm sorry it's slushy when it's going.

Ogden Nash

TREES
The leaves have long since fallen off the maple tree, but there are still a few "helicopters" here and there. Snow lies on some of the bigger branches. The tree is resting for the winter and is well provided for.

BIRDS
A blackbird sits on a low branch of the maple tree. Some small birds look for insects hidden in cracks in the tree. There are great tits, a few blue tits, a nuthatch and a woodpecker.

   A few crows caw, a lone magpie hops on the ground, a robin sits on the fence, but there aren't many birds about.

PLANTS
Heather and cowberries are still green but most other plants have withered. Only the dry stalk of a cow parsley remains and the burdock is brown with a few prickly fruit left. They release their seeds in the winter which the hungry birds eat.

INSECTS
There are insects hiding in cracks in the bark of the maple and other trees and the birds hunt for them eagerly. It is rare to see an insect outside.

OTHER ANIMALS
The hare leaps over the snow in its brown fur. It is easy to spot and has no protection apart from its speed.

   Mice, voles and shrews live under the snow. Sometimes you can find the tracks on the snow.

Tracks in the snow

This is how a mouse eats: It is a neat eater. The cone is stripped clean and only the core remains.

This is how a squirrel eats: It holds the pine cone tightly and gnaws both scales and seeds. The cone looks a bit sloppily eaten.

This is how a woodpecker eats: It pecks violently at the cones to pick out the seeds. The cones get totally demolished.

HARE

DEER

TYPICAL HARE DROPPINGS!

Nicky has learned to identify different animals' tracks and other signs, such as droppings and food remains. There are all sorts of clues that animals leave behind even in winter. Pine cones are eaten by lots of animals and you can tell who has eaten them by the remains. Woodpeckers wedge their cones into a crack in a tree before eating them. Beneath the tree there are usually large piles of cones that have fallen down. Hazelnuts with large holes in them can be found

...AND WHO'S DONE A POO HERE?

FOX

SQUIRREL

ELK

wedged in cracks in a tree.

Mice and voles make neat round holes in nuts with clear teeth marks.

Squirrels crack nuts in half and leave the shell behind.

Feet leave tracks
You can often see hare tracks. Hares hide in their open nests, called forms, in the daytime. They make clear foot prints and you can get quite close to one before it runs away. Rabbit tracks are the same as hare's but smaller.

Fox prints wind through the fields and along ditches. Dog and fox tracks are quite alike.

Squirrels leave tracks on the ground when it's too far to hop between the trees.

You can see the drag mark of a rodent's tail between its footprints. The elk leaves clear footprints; those belonging to the deer are smaller. Nicky spots hare droppings here and there. Elk and deer droppings look similar to a hare's but they are, of course, larger!

The fox leaves its droppings on top of a rock or tree stump. It is less likely to be surprised by an enemy there.

SOMETIMES YOU'RE LUCKY

Plants,

Most plants wither away but their roots live on underground. Other plants lose their leaves. Only the evergreens provide colour against the snow. Pine trees survive the cold well and so does heather because its thick leaves are covered with waxy layers. Nicky scratches a leaf with her nail and looks at it under a magnifying glass.

Under the snow the buds are ready for next year's flowering.

Why don't flowers bloom?
Sometimes in the midst of winter there are warm sunny days. But the flowers still don't blossom!

All plants need a winter's rest before the buds can start to develop. You can test this by taking in twigs of birch or hazel. Start at Christmas time and continue picking a twig a week throughout the winter. The first branches won't do anything but eventually you will see the buds start to open.

Look at a wasp's nest!
Nicky has taken down the wasp's nest in the attic. Next year's wasps will build a new one anyway. They are beautifully built with different storeys and columns in between. The nest is light but strong. It is made of chewed up wood – just like papier mâché.

When the winds blow hard, the birds stand on the ice with their beaks facing the wind. Standing this way their feathers are pressed against their bodies and no cold air can get through. Otherwise the wind would ruffle their feathers and squeeze out the warm air, next to their bodies. They would freeze!

Don't their feet freeze?
Birds have very few blood vessels in their legs. They can close some of them off if it gets too cold. Then there isn't so much blood to cool down.

animals and winter

The tawny owl
hunts at night. It can see very well even in little light, but it hears even better. No rodent moving under the snow is safe. Suddenly, the owl pounces.

Owls fly silently because their wing feathers are fringed on the outer edge and the air filters through the fringes.

Bees keep each other warm
Bees spend the winter in their hives. They huddle together to keep warm. If it gets too cold, they fan their wings, which increases the heat. The temperature in the hive never goes below 12°C even in a truly cold winter.

Animals under the snow
A thick blanket of snow is the best protection against cold that either an animal or plant can have. In the space between the snow and the ground the temperature is near 0°C.

Take some leaves home!
Nicky digs underneath the snow and takes home a bag full of dead leaves. She places them on a tray. At first nothing stirs, but after a while the small animals wake up. The leaf litter is teeming with life!

OH ME! OH MY!

Help animals to survive the winter

If the winter is hard, many animals have a difficult time. Many birds look to people to get food. Why don't you make a bird table for them. It isn't difficult to do.

On the table put sunflower seeds, hemp seeds and oats, not just bread crusts. The bread should not be mouldy!

Melt some suet or fat together with chopped nuts, sunflower seeds and grain. When it has cooled, place the mixture in bags made of netting and hang them up in a tree or bush. Put apples under the bird table – the blackbirds (and mice!) will love them. In the autumn Nicky picked bunches of rowan berries and kept them in her freezer. Now that it is cold and there's little food she hangs them from twigs for the birds.

You can make a simple seed dispenser. Cut some holes in the side of a plastic bucket near the bottom. Place it on a tree stump. (To get a larger dining table you could hammer a piece of plywood, or an old tray on top of the stump.) Put a lid on top of the bucket to keep the rain out. A bucket full of seeds will last at least two weeks.

But remember! If you have started giving the animals food, you must continue until spring comes.

It's very exciting to watch all the birds. Nicky has seen house sparrows, tree sparrows, great tits, greenfinches, blue tits, bullfinches, waxwings and blackbirds. Have you seen more?

HELP YOURSELVES TEA'S READY!

DO YOU WANT TO READ FURTHER?

There are lots of nature books. It's good to take a field guide to birds and one to flowers along with you.

Collins Handguides
Well laid-out guides to birds, flowers, trees, wild animals, butterflies etc. Easy to follow.

Collins Gems
Inexpensive, well-illustrated, pocket-sized guides on a wide range of subjects.

Usborne Nature Trail Series
Good introductions for young wild-life enthusiasts to the art of observing nature.

Usborne Spotter's Guides
Tell you what to look out for and how to identify what you have found in various habitats.